Common Sense *Cooking*

The Wildtree Cookbook Collection

Common Sense *Cooking*

The Wildtree Cookbook Collection

Published by Wildtree Herbs, Inc.

Copyright © 2005 by
Wildtree Herbs, Inc.
11 Knight Street
Warwick, Rhode Island 02886
401-732-1856
www.wildtreeherbs.com

Photographs © by Mark Taulbee Photography

Edited, Designed, and Manufactured by
Favorite Recipes® Press
an Imprint of

FRP

P.O. Box 305142
Nashville, Tennessee 37230
800-358-0560

Art Director: Steve Newman
Book Design: Starletta Polster
Project Editor: Tanis Westbrook

Manufactured in China
First Printing: 2005
25,000 copies

table of contents

the inspiration

Until the mid 90s, Leslie Montie never dreamed she would become the founder of a company that helps families enjoy great-tasting, nutritious meals that can be prepared in minutes. Leslie's two young children had recently been diagnosed with medical conditions that required restricted diets. "It was amazing how this impacted our entire family," recalls Leslie. "I needed to come up with meals that everyone would enjoy with ingredients my children wouldn't react to. And since I was a full-time working mom, they had to be easy to make."

Leslie sought the help of her parents, Frank and Judy. As concerned parents and grandparents, Frank and Judy immediately began experimenting with new ways to flavor and prepare foods. "It was really a hit-and-miss sort of process, and we came up with some great ideas," says Leslie.

"I remember thinking that others would benefit from what we discovered—how to make mealtime an enjoyable and effortless experience, dietary restrictions or not!" And this sincere desire to help others was the inspiration that led Leslie to found Wildtree Herbs in 1996.

Leslie and her mom, Judy, began by selling their specialty blends at local craft fairs. They were overwhelmed by the reception and quickly gained a loyal following. When an enthusiastic customer asked Leslie if she had considered selling exclusively through home parties, she loved the idea! "I held my first party a few weeks later and knew it was the ideal way to bring our products to families across the country!" In 1999, Wildtree Herbs, Inc., was officially launched as a party plan company.

the creations

Every Wildtree product is natural,

containing no additives,

preservatives, MSG, or food dyes.

"We oversee every step

of the process in-house." says Leslie.

"From research to development,

manufacturing to delivery, we seek to

provide the best products and

quality service our customers deserve."

WILDTREE HERBS

Lighter *Fare*

Roasted Red Bell Pepper Bruschetta

Serves 8

1 loaf French bread, sliced on the diagonal
Wildtree Roasted Garlic Grapeseed Oil
1/3 cup Wildtree Roasted Red Bell Pepper Pesto Blend
1/4 cup warm water
1/4 cup Wildtree Roasted Garlic Grapeseed Oil

Brush the bread slices with Roasted Garlic Grapeseed Oil and arrange on a baking sheet. Bake at 350 degrees until light brown. Combine the Roasted Red Bell Pepper Pesto Blend with the warm water in a bowl and mix well. Add 1/4 cup Roasted Garlic Grapeseed Oil and mix well, adding additional oil if necessary to reach the desired consistency. Spread on the toasted bread slices.

Serve with Parmesan cheese shavings. You may substitute Wildtree Natural Grapeseed Oil for the Roasted Garlic Grapeseed Oil if desired.

Pot Stickers with Asian Sauce

Serves 6 to 12

1 package frozen pot stickers
1/2 cup Wildtree Asian Sauce, warm or at room temperature

Cook the pot stickers using the package directions. Pour the Asian Sauce into a dipping dish.

Serve with the pot stickers. You may substitute egg rolls for the pot stickers if desired and Wildtree Asian Ginger Plum Sauce for the Asian Sauce.

scampi blend stuffed mushrooms

Serves 8

1 sleeve butter crackers, crushed
10 tablespoons (1 1/4 sticks) butter, melted
2 tablespoons Wildtree Scampi Blend
1/4 teaspoon lemon juice
4 ounces any combination of scallops, crab meat, lobster or shrimp, finely chopped
1 1/4 pounds mushroom caps

Combine the crackers, butter, Scampi Blend and lemon juice in a bowl and mix well. Add the seafood and mix well. Arrange the mushroom caps on a baking sheet. Spoon the seafood mixture into the mushroom caps. Bake at 350 degrees for 7 to 10 minutes or until heated through and light brown on top.

Wildtree Tip: *Sprinkle a tablespoon of the Scampi Blend over a bowl of popcorn.*

tomato salad

Serves 8

2 tomatoes, finely chopped
3/4 large sweet onion, such as Vidalia, Spanish or Bermuda, finely chopped
1/4 cup Wildtree Balsamic Vinaigrette Dressing & Marinade
4 bagels

Combine the tomatoes, onion and Balsamic Vinaigrette Dressing & Marinade in a bowl and mix gently. Let stand for 1 hour. Cut the bagels into halves and arrange in a shallow pan. Bake until lightly toasted. Spoon the tomato mixture over the bagels and chill, covered, for 1 hour. Cut the bagels into quarters and serve.

You may substitute French bread or any crusty bread, cut lengthwise and toasted, for the bagels.

smoked salmon spread

Serves 8

1 tablespoon Wildtree Smoked Salmon Blend
1 tablespoon warm water
8 ounces cream cheese, softened
Chopped green onions or chives to taste (optional)

Combine the Smoked Salmon Blend and water in a small bowl and mix well. Let stand for 2 to 3 minutes. Add the cream cheese and stir until blended. Add green onions and mix well. Let stand for 1 hour to allow the flavors to blend.

Serve as a spread for bagels or crackers.

spinach & leek blend spread

Serves 8

3 tablespoons Wildtree Spinach & Leek Blend
3 tablespoons warm water
8 ounces cream cheese, softened

Combine the Spinach & Leek Blend and water in a small bowl and mix well. Let stand until the water is absorbed. Add the cream cheese and stir until blended. Chill, covered, for 1 hour to allow the flavors to blend.

Serve as a spread for bagels or crackers, stuff into celery, whip into mashed potatoes or use as a sandwich spread.

***Wildtree Tip:** You may also combine the Spinach & Leek Blend with sour cream and use as a vegetable dip or as a topping for baked potatoes, or combine with Wildtree Natural Grapeseed Oil and melted butter and toss with red potatoes.*

DILL DIP
Serves 8

½ cup mayonnaise
½ cup sour cream
2 teaspoons Wildtree Dill Dip Blend
1½ teaspoons lemon juice (optional)

Combine the mayonnaise and sour cream in a bowl and stir until blended. Add the Dill Dip Blend and lemon juice and mix well. Chill, covered, until ready to serve.

Serve with apples, broccoli, cauliflower, celery, nectarines, peppers, rye crackers, shrimp, green beans, zucchini or baked potatoes.

Serve as a substitute for tartar sauce with fish or as a sandwich spread in place of mayonnaise. Brush on fish or pork before grilling or baking.

Wildtree Tip: *You may also combine a small amount of the Dill Dip Blend with Wildtree Natural Grapeseed Oil and white wine and use as a marinade for fish, pork or veal.*

🍃 *Combine with oil and vinegar for a great salad dressing.*
🍃 *Sprinkle the Dill Dip Blend on vegetables before cooking.*

Garlic & Herb Blend

Serves 8

1 tablespoon Wildtree Garlic & Herb Blend
8 ounces cream cheese, softened

Combine the Garlic & Herb Blend and cream cheese in a small bowl and mix until blended. Chill, covered, until ready to serve.

Serve with crackers or vegetables, as a spread for bagels or add to mashed potatoes. You may substitute sour cream or yogurt for half the cream cheese as a variation.

For a low-fat version, use low-fat cream cheese, nonfat or low-fat sour cream or nonfat yogurt.

Wildtree Tip: *Combine the Garlic & Herb Blend with sour cream and use on baked potatoes.*

🌿 *Combine the Garlic & Herb Blend with butter and spread on Italian bread, or combine with Wildtree Natural Grapeseed Oil and vinegar for a great salad dressing.*

🌿 *Combine 1 teaspoon Garlic & Herb Blend with 2 tablespoons mayonnaise and brush on swordfish, tuna or your favorite fish before grilling.*

🌿 *Combine 1 teaspoon Garlic & Herb Blend with ¼ cup Wildtree Natural Grapeseed Oil and brush on steak, pork or poultry and let stand for 30 minutes. Grill to the desired degree of doneness. You may also use to brush on vegetables before grilling or roasting.*

🌿 *Use the Garlic & Herb Blend to season spaghetti sauces, or combine with Wildtree Natural Grapeseed Oil and toss with pasta.*

Jalapeño Pepper Blend

Serves 8

2 tablespoons Wildtree Jalapeño Pepper Blend
1 tablespoon warm water
8 ounces cream cheese, softened

Combine the Jalapeño Pepper Blend with the water in a small bowl and mix well. Let stand for 5 minutes. Add the cream cheese and mix until blended. Let stand for 1 hour before serving.

Serve as a spread for crackers, bagels, English muffins, toast or bread or as a stuffing for celery. Serve as a sandwich spread in place of mayonnaise.

Wildtree Tip: *Combine the Jalapeño Pepper Blend with sour cream and serve with nachos. Combine the rehydrated Jalapeño Pepper Blend with Wildtree Natural Grapeseed Oil, toss with cooked pasta and heat.*

mesquite smoked
sun-dried tomato &
leek blend

Serves 8

1 tablespoon Wildtree Mesquite Smoked Sun-Dried Tomato & Leek Blend
1 tablespoon warm water
8 ounces cream cheese, softened

Combine the Mesquite Smoked Sun-Dried Tomato & Leek Blend with the water in a small bowl and mix well. Let stand for 5 minutes. Add the cream cheese and mix until blended. Let stand for 1 hour before serving.

Serve as a spread for crackers, bagels, English muffins and toast or as a stuffing for celery.

Wildtree Tip: Combine the Mesquite Smoked Sun-Dried Tomato & Leek Blend with Wildtree Natural Grapeseed Oil and toss with cooked pasta.

breakfast ideas

Toast sprinkled with *Wildtree Cinnamon Sugar*

Try one of the following spreads on a toasted bagel:

Garlic & Herb Spread

Smoked Salmon Spread

Confetti Veggie Spread

Cranberry Horseradish Spread

Cranberry Spice Spread

Mesquite Smoked Sun-Dried Tomato & Leek Spread

Red Bell Pepper & Garlic Spread

Jalapeño Pepper Spread

Spinach & Leek Spread

Serve an English muffin with:

Mesquite Smoked Sun-Dried Tomato & Leek Spread, fried egg and cheese

Smoked Salmon Dip, sliced red onion, capers and fresh mozzarella

Jalapeño Pepper Spread, black beans or refried beans, sliced green onions,
avocado, sour cream and salsa.

Use a pinch of *Wildtree Cajun Seasoning* as a flavor enhancer in scrambled or fried eggs
or in an omelet.

Add *Wildtree Cranberry Spice Blend*, *Wildtree Apple Pie Spice Blend*, or *Wildtree Pumpkin
Pie Spice Blend* to your pancake or waffle batter.

slaw with wildtree asian ginger-plum dressing & marinade

Serves 4

2 cups broccoli slaw
1/2 cup cashews
1/4 to 1/2 cup Wildtree Asian Ginger-Plum Dressing & Marinade

Combine the broccoli slaw, cashews and Asian Ginger-Plum Dressing & Marinade in a bowl and mix well. Chill before serving.

oven fries

Serves 4

4 Yukon gold or russet potatoes
2 tablespoons Wildtree Roasted Garlic Grapeseed Oil or Natural Grapeseed Oil
1 tablespoon Wildtree Cajun Seasoning or Wildtree Buffalo Wing Marinade
Salt and freshly ground pepper to taste

Cut the potatoes lengthwise into thick slices. Cut each slice into 1/2 x 1/2-inch-thick pieces. Combine with cold water to cover in a bowl and let stand for a few minutes. Drain and thoroughly dry with paper towels.

Toss the potatoes with the Roasted Garlic Grapeseed Oil in a bowl. Arrange the potatoes in a single layer in a dark roasting pan or on a baking sheet. Sprinkle with the Cajun Seasoning or Buffalo Wing Marinade, salt and pepper.

Bake at 425 degrees for 35 to 40 minutes or until brown and crisp, turning occasionally. Serve immediately.

wildtree's home fries

Serves 4

1 pound potatoes
Butter or margarine
Wildtree Roasted Garlic Grapeseed Oil or Wildtree Natural Grapeseed Oil
1 teaspoon Wildtree Home Fries Seasoning

Cut the potatoes lengthwise into halves. Combine the potatoes with water to cover in a large saucepan. Simmer until almost cooked through but still firm. Cut the potatoes into thick slices.

Combine equal amounts of butter and Roasted Garlic Grapeseed Oil with the Home Fries Seasoning in a skillet. Add the potatoes and cook to the desired degree of doneness. You may try this with other firm vegetables, such as broccoli, green beans or onions.

Wildtree Tip: *Prepare the home fries in advance and chill in the refrigerator. Heat the potatoes just before serving.*

Bloody mary potatoes

Serves 4

4 red potatoes, cut into 1-inch pieces
1 tablespoon butter
1 tablespoon Wildtree Natural Grapeseed Oil or Roasted Garlic Grapeseed Oil
1 teaspoon Wildtree Blasted Bloody Mary Mix
Chopped fresh flat-leaf parsley

Combine the potatoes with water to cover in a saucepan. Simmer until the potatoes are tender; drain. Combine the butter and Natural Grapeseed Oil in a small saucepan and heat until the butter is melted. Add the Blasted Bloody Mary Mix and mix well. Combine with the potatoes in a bowl and toss gently. Sprinkle with parsley and serve immediately.

potato panache

Makes a variable amount

Wildtree Mesquite Smoked Sun-Dried Tomato & Leek Blend
Mashed potatoes
Sliced green onions
Dash of pepper
Cornmeal
Butter or margarine

Rehydrate Mesquite Smoked Sun-Dried Tomato & Leek Blend using the package directions. Combine with potatoes, green onions and pepper in a bowl and mix well. Shape the mixture into 1-inch-thick patties and coat lightly with cornmeal.

Melt a small amount of butter in a nonstick skillet. Fry the patties in the butter until brown and crisp, turning once.

Wildtree Tip: *Fill your salt shaker with Wildtree Lemon Pepper Blend and use in place of salt. It is especially delicious sprinkled on vegetables.*

garlic & herb blend twice-baked potatoes

Serves 4

4 potatoes
1 tablespoon butter
Milk
1 tablespoon Wildtree Garlic & Herb Blend
1/2 cup (2 ounces) shredded Cheddar cheese

Bake the potatoes at 400 degrees for 45 minutes. Cut the potatoes lengthwise into halves. Scoop the pulp from the potatoes into a bowl, reserving the shells. Add the butter and desired amount of milk to the pulp and mash. Add the Garlic & Herb Blend and mix well. Spoon the mixture into the reserved shells and sprinkle with the cheese. Arrange on a baking sheet.

Bake at 350 degrees until the cheese is bubbly.

cajun vegetables

Makes a variable amount

Wildtree Cajun Seasoning to taste
Fresh vegetables, chopped

Sprinkle Cajun Seasoning on vegetables. Steam or grill the vegetables to the desired degree of doneness.

You may also combine the vegetables with your favorite Wildtree Grapeseed Oil and Cajun Seasoning in a large bowl and toss gently. Place the vegetables on a piece of aluminum foil. Cook over medium-hot coals to the desired degree of doneness, turning often.

DILLY VEGETABLES

Makes a variable amount

Fresh vegetables, chopped
Wildtree Dill Dip Blend to taste

Steam or grill vegetables to the desired degree of doneness. Sprinkle with Dill Dip Blend and serve immediately.

Wildtree Tip: *Never season vegetables with salt during cooking. The salt will draw out the liquid and they will not cook evenly.*

OLD-FASHIONED STUFFING

Serves 8

½ cup (1 stick) butter
2 cups chopped celery
2 cups chopped onion
2 tablespoons Wildtree Poultry Seasoning
1 loaf bread, cubed
1 cup coarsely chopped walnuts
Water or chicken broth

Melt the butter over medium heat in a roasting pan. Add the celery and onion and cook until translucent, stirring frequently. Add the Poultry Seasoning, bread cubes and walnuts and cook until the bread cubes are light brown, stirring frequently and adding water as needed to reach the desired consistency. Bake at 325 to 350 degrees for 1 hour. This recipe may easily be doubled.

family *Favorites*

Lemon Pepper Chicken

Serves 4

1 tablespoon Wildtree Lemon Pepper Blend
2 tablespoons Wildtree Natural Grapeseed Oil
1 1/2 pounds boneless skinless chicken breasts, or 2 whole chicken breasts cut into halves

Combine the Lemon Pepper Blend and Natural Grapeseed Oil in a small bowl. Brush the mixture on the chicken. Grill the chicken over high heat for 2 minutes on each side. Reduce the heat to low and grill until the juices run clear when pierced with a fork.

Remove from the heat and let stand, covered with aluminum foil, for 3 to 5 minutes. Serve whole or sliced on the diagonal.

You may bake at 325 degrees, broil or fry the chicken if preferred.

Basil Pesto Chicken

Serves 4

1 tablespoon Wildtree Basil Pesto Blend
3 tablespoons warm water
2 tablespoons Wildtree Natural Grapeseed Oil
1 1/2 pounds boneless skinless chicken breasts, or 2 whole chicken breasts cut into halves

Combine the Basil Pesto Blend with the water in a small bowl and mix well. Let stand until the water is absorbed. Add the Natural Grapeseed Oil and mix well. Brush the mixture over the chicken.

Grill over high heat for 2 minutes on each side. Reduce the heat to low and grill until the juices run clear when pierced with a fork. Remove from the heat and let stand, covered with aluminum foil, for 3 to 5 minutes. Serve whole or slice on the diagonal. You may substitute boneless skinless chicken thighs for the chicken breasts if desired. You may bake at 325 degrees, broil or fry the chicken if preferred.

GRILLED CAJUN CHICKEN BREAST

Serves 4

1 tablespoon Wildtree Cajun Seasoning
1 1/2 tablespoons Wildtree Natural Grapeseed Oil
4 boneless skinless chicken breasts

Combine the Cajun Seasoning and Natural Grapeseed Oil in a shallow dish and mix well. Add the chicken and marinate for 30 minutes or longer. Grill over medium heat until the chicken tests done, turning occasionally.

Wildtree Tip: *For a blackened taste, add a little more Natural Grapeseed Oil to the Cajun Seasoning and fry the chicken in a hot skillet.*

CHICKEN SALAD WITH RED BELL PEPPER & GARLIC

Serves 4

1 tablespoon Wildtree Red Bell Pepper & Garlic Blend
1 tablespoon water
2 cups chopped cooked chicken
2 green onions, thinly sliced
1/4 cup mayonnaise
1/4 cup sour cream
Salt and pepper to taste
Sliced cucumber

Combine the Red Bell Pepper & Garlic Blend and water in a small bowl and mix well. Let stand for 3 to 5 minutes. Combine with the chicken, green onions, mayonnaise and sour cream in a bowl and mix well. Season with salt and pepper. Serve with sliced cucumber.

scampi chicken with rice

Serves 4

4 boneless skinless chicken breasts
1 tablespoon butter or margarine
2 teaspoons Wildtree Scampi Blend
1/4 cup milk
1 tablespoon butter or margarine
2 teaspoons Wildtree Scampi Blend
1 tablespoon flour
Salt and pepper to taste
Hot cooked rice

Cut the chicken into bite-size pieces. Melt 1 tablespoon butter in a skillet over medium heat. Add 2 teaspoons Scampi Blend and the chicken and sauté until the chicken is cooked through. Add the milk, 1 tablespoon butter, 2 teaspoons Scampi Blend and the flour and cook until thickened, stirring constantly. Season with salt and pepper. Serve over rice.

rotisserie chicken

Serves 4

2 1/2 teaspoons Wildtree Rotisserie Chicken Blend
1/2 cup flour
4 chicken breasts or boneless chicken breasts
Wildtree Natural Grapeseed Oil

Combine the Rotisserie Chicken Blend and flour in a shallow dish and mix well. Dredge the chicken in the flour mixture. Heat a small amount of Natural Grapeseed Oil in a skillet. Add the chicken and cook until cooked through, turning occasionally.

You may substitute pork for the chicken if desired.

fajitas

Makes 9 to 12 fajitas

1/4 cup Wildtree Fajita Seasoning Blend
1/2 cup water
1 1/2 pounds boneless skinless chicken breasts,
cut into 1/2-inch strips
1 to 2 tablespoons Wildtree Natural Grapeseed Oil
2 onions, sliced
2 green or red bell peppers, sliced
2 tablespoons Wildtree Natural Grapeseed Oil
9 to 12 tortillas
Shredded Cheddar cheese
Chopped tomatoes
Chopped iceberg lettuce
Chopped black olives
Wildtree Chunky Style Salsa
Sour cream
Guacamole

Wildtree Tip:
You may substitute 1 1/2 pounds flank steak, shrimp or thick, firm white fish for the chicken if desired. If using flank steak, marinate for 1 hour.

Combine the Fajita Seasoning Blend with the water in a dish and mix well. Add the chicken and let stand for 20 minutes; drain and discard the marinade.

Heat 1 to 2 tablespoons Natural Grapeseed Oil in a large skillet. Add the onions and bell peppers and cook until soft, stirring frequently. Remove to a serving dish and cover to keep warm.

Heat 2 tablespoons Natural Grapeseed Oil in the skillet. Add the chicken and sauté until cooked through.

Place the tortillas on a baking sheet. Warm at 250 degrees. Wrap the warm tortillas in a clean, dry kitchen towel. Serve the tortillas with the chicken, bell pepper mixture, cheese, tomatoes, lettuce, olives, salsa, sour cream and guacamole. This makes a great fajita salad too.

RIB-eye steaks with wildtree rancher steak rub & seasoning and wildtree's mashed potatoes

Serves 4

1 tablespoon Wildtree Garlic & Herb Blend
8 ounces cream cheese, softened
2 pounds Yukon gold potatoes, cut into 1 ½-inch pieces
4 rib-eye steaks
Wildtree Natural Grapeseed Oil or Wildtree Roasted Garlic Grapeseed Oil
Wildtree Rancher Steak Rub & Seasoning to taste
2 tablespoons butter

Combine the Garlic & Herb Blend with the cream cheese in a bowl and mix until blended. Chill, covered, for 2 hours. Combine the potatoes with water to cover in a saucepan and bring to a boil. Reduce the heat and simmer for 20 to 25 minutes or until the potatoes are tender; drain.

Rub the steaks with Natural Grapeseed Oil and sprinkle with Rancher Steak Rub & Seasoning. Press the Rancher Steak Rub & Seasoning into the steaks. Grill over hot coals until almost to the desired degree of doneness, turning once. Remove the steaks to a platter and let rest, covered with aluminum foil, for a few minutes.

Combine the butter with ½ cup of the Garlic & Herb Blend mixture in a small saucepan over low heat and cook just until heated through, stirring frequently. Mash the potatoes in a bowl. Add half of the heated Garlic & Herb Blend mixture and mix well, adding additional Garlic & Herb Blend mixture if necessary.

Serve the steaks with the potatoes and a green salad. The remaining Garlic & Herb Blend mixture may be used as a spread for crackers.

deanne's stew

Serves 8

1 1/2 pounds stew beef, cubed
3 potatoes, chopped
1 onion, finely chopped
8 ounces carrots, sliced
1 cup frozen vegetables, such as green beans and mustard greens
1/2 cup flour
1 tablespoon Wildtree Scampi Blend
1 tablespoon Wildtree Roasted Garlic Grapeseed Oil
4 cups beef broth

Combine the beef, potatoes, onion, carrots, frozen vegetables, flour, Scampi Blend, Roasted Garlic Grapeseed Oil and broth in a slow cooker and cook on Low for 8 hours. You may also brown the beef in the Roasted Garlic Grapeseed Oil in a stockpot. Add the remaining ingredients and simmer for 2 hours.

> ***Wildtree Tip:*** *To thicken stews, add a small amount of quick-cooking oats or grated potato.*

justin's hearty roast beef sandwiches

Serves 4

1 1/2 teaspoons Wildtree Garlic & Herb Blend
4 ounces cream cheese, softened
8 slices marble rye bread
1 pound roast beef, sliced
8 ounces bacon, crisp-cooked
Lettuce
Sliced tomato

Combine the Garlic & Herb Blend with the cream cheese in a small bowl and mix until blended. Spread an equal amount of the mixture on 4 slices of the bread. Top with the roast beef, bacon, lettuce, tomato slices and remaining slices of bread. Cut into quarters and serve immediately.

THE BEST BURGER
Serves 4

1 pound ground beef, ground turkey or ground chicken
1/2 teaspoon Wildtree Cajun Seasoning
1/2 teaspoon Wildtree Rancher Steak Rub & Seasoning

Shape the ground beef into 4 patties. Sprinkle 1 side of the patties with the Cajun Seasoning and press into the patties. Sprinkle the other side of the patties with the Rancher Steak Rub & Seasoning and press into the patties. Grill over hot coals or fry in a skillet to the desired degree of doneness, turning once.

LESLIE'S CHILI
Serves 6

Wildtree Tip:
A pinch or 2 of Wildtree Cajun Seasoning is a flavor enhancer for casseroles, soups, and stews. For an added kick, try Wildtree Flamin Cajun Seasoning.

2 pounds ground beef or ground turkey
6 tablespoons Wildtree Leslie's Chili Mix
1 (28-ounce) can crushed tomatoes
1 cup water
1/2 teaspoon cayenne pepper, or crushed red pepper to taste
(optional)
1 (15-ounce) can kidney beans (optional)
Shredded Cheddar cheese (optional)
Sour cream (optional)

Brown the ground beef in a skillet, stirring until crumbly; drain. Combine the Leslie's Chili Mix, tomatoes and water in a large saucepan over medium-high heat and bring to a boil. Add the ground beef and reduce the heat to low. Simmer for 15 minutes, stirring occasionally. Add the cayenne pepper and kidney beans and cook until heated through. Serve with Cheddar cheese and sour cream.

veal cutlets with wildtree Lemon rosemary blend

Serves 4

½ cup unseasoned bread crumbs
1 tablespoon Wildtree Lemon Rosemary Blend
1 pound veal cutlets, pounded thin
1 egg, beaten
2 tablespoons Wildtree Natural Grapeseed Oil or Wildtree Zesty Lemon Grapeseed Oil

Combine the bread crumbs and Lemon Rosemary Blend in a shallow dish and mix well. Dip the veal in the egg and coat with the bread crumb mixture.

Sauté the veal in the Natural Grapeseed Oil in a skillet until the juices run clear when pierced with a fork, turning occasionally. Remove from the heat and let stand, covered with aluminum foil, for 3 to 5 minutes.

baby back ribs with wildtree memphis barbeque rub

Serves 4

2 to 4 pounds baby back ribs
Wildtree Natural Grapeseed Oil
Wildtree Memphis Barbeque Rub or Hot Memphis Barbeque Rub
Wildtree Memphis Barbeque Dipping & Finishing Sauce

Rub the ribs with the Natural Grapeseed Oil. Sprinkle with the Memphis Barbeque Rub. Press the rub into the ribs. Sear the ribs on the grill over high heat, turning once.

Turn off the heat on half the grill. Move the ribs to the cooler edge of the grill and grill, with the lid closed, for 2 to 3 hours or until the meat is tender and pulling away from the bone. Brush the Memphis Barbeque Dipping & Finishing Sauce on the ribs. Grill for 5 minutes on each side. Serve with broccoli slaw mixed with Wildtree Asian Ginger-Plum Dressing & Marinade.

herb grilled pork
Serves 4

2 tablespoons Wildtree Herb Grilling Marinade
2 tablespoons Wildtree Natural Grapeseed Oil
1 1/2 pounds boneless pork cutlets or boneless pork chops

Combine the Herb Grilling Marinade and Natural Grapeseed Oil in a shallow bowl and whisk until blended. Add the pork and turn to coat both sides with the mixture. Marinate for 20 minutes; discard the marinade.

Grill the pork over medium-high heat for 2 minutes on each side. Reduce the heat to low and grill until the juices run clear when pierced with a fork. Remove to a platter and let stand, covered with aluminum foil, for 3 to 5 minutes.

Serve whole or slice on the diagonal. You may bake at 350 degrees, fry or broil the pork instead of grilling if desired.

Wildtree Tip: For a handy, nearly already prepared entrée, combine all the ingredients in a sealable plastic bag and shake until the pork is coated. Place the bag in the freezer until ready to use. Remove from the freezer in the morning, and it will be ready to cook in the evening!

Lamb chops with wildtree Lemon rosemary blend

Serves 4

2 tablespoons Wildtree Lemon Rosemary Blend
1 cup panko or unseasoned bread crumbs
3 to 4 pounds lamb chops
1 tablespoon Wildtree Natural Grapeseed Oil or Wildtree Zesty Lemon Grapeseed Oil

Combine the Lemon Rosemary Blend and panko in a shallow dish. Brush the lamb chops with the Natural Grapeseed Oil and coat with the panko mixture. Place the prepared lamb chops in a baking dish.

Bake at 350 degrees until the desired degree of doneness.

Grilled salmon with dill

Serves 4

1/2 cup mayonnaise
1/2 cup sour cream
2 teaspoons Wildtree Dill Dip Blend
1 pound salmon fillets or salmon steaks

Combine the mayonnaise, sour cream and Dill Dip Blend in a bowl and mix well. Chill, covered, in the refrigerator.

Grill the salmon, skin side down, over medium heat until opaque in the center. Remove to dinner plates. Top with the Dill Dip Blend mixture or serve on the side. Serve with lemon wedges. If grilling salmon steaks, turn the steaks once during the grilling process.

wildtree asian sauce with shrimp and pasta

Serves 4

1 pound shrimp, shelled and deveined
1 tablespoon Wildtree Asian Sauce
2 red bell peppers, cut into 1-inch pieces
8 green onions, sliced on the diagonal
1 tablespoon Wildtree Natural Grapeseed Oil
½ cup Wildtree Asian Sauce
16 ounces penne pasta, cooked

Marinate the shrimp in 1 tablespoon Asian Sauce for 20 minutes. Sauté the shrimp in a nonstick skillet over medium heat until the shrimp curl and turn pink. Remove to a bowl and cover to keep warm.

Sauté the bell peppers and green onions in the Natural Grapeseed Oil in a skillet until softened. Add ½ cup Asian Sauce and the shrimp and cook until heated through. Combine with the pasta in a bowl and serve immediately.

You may substitute scallops or sliced chicken for the shrimp if desired.

Wildtree Tip: *For a variation, replace the bell peppers with shredded carrots, snow peas, and whole peanuts. Serve over thin rice noodles with sprigs of fresh cilantro.*

SHRIMP SALAD

Serves 4

1 pound medium shrimp, cooked, shelled and deveined
1/4 cup finely chopped celery
1 tablespoon chopped chives
1 tablespoon mayonnaise
1 teaspoon Wildtree Dill Dip Blend

Chop the shrimp. Combine the shrimp with the celery, chives, mayonnaise and Dill Dip Blend in a bowl and mix well.

Chill slightly before serving. Serve over a bed of lettuce.

SHRIMP AND SHELLS

Serves 2

1 1/4 cups small seashell pasta
4 ounces fresh snow peas
8 ounces shrimp, cooked
2 to 3 tablespoons Wildtree Natural Grapeseed Oil
1 garlic clove, minced
1 teaspoon Wildtree Dill Dip Blend
1/3 cup freshly grated Parmesan cheese

Cook the pasta using the package directions; drain. Steam the snow peas until tender-crisp. Combine the shrimp, Natural Grapeseed oil, garlic and Dill Dip Blend in a small skillet and cook over medium heat until hot. Add the pasta, snow peas and cheese and toss to coat.

shrimp scampi

Serves 2 as an entrée or 4 as an appetizer

8 ounces linguini or your choice of pasta
2 tablespoons Wildtree Natural Grapeseed Oil or Wildtree Roasted Garlic Grapeseed Oil
1 1/2 teaspoons Wildtree Scampi Blend
1 pound shrimp, shelled and deveined
2 tablespoons Wildtree Natural Grapeseed Oil or Wildtree Roasted Garlic Grapeseed Oil
1 teaspoon Wildtree Scampi Blend
Dry white wine (optional)

Cook the pasta using the package directions; drain, reserving 1/4 cup of the liquid. Combine 2 tablespoons Natural Grapeseed Oil and 1 1/2 teaspoons Scampi Blend in a cold skillet and mix well. Add the shrimp and cook over medium-low heat until the shrimp turn pink, turning often. Remove the shrimp to a bowl using a slotted spoon and keep warm.

Add 2 tablespoons Natural Grapeseed Oil and 1 teaspoon Scampi Blend to the liquid in the skillet. Add the pasta and cook over low heat until the liquid is absorbed, adding the reserved pasta liquid or dry white wine if the pasta seems too dry. Combine the pasta and shrimp in a bowl and serve immediately.

pizza topping ideas

*Crushed tomatoes, shredded mozzarella cheese and
Wildtree Hearty Spaghetti Sauce Blend*

Fresh tomatoes, Wildtree Basil Pesto and grated Parmesan cheese

*Crushed tomatoes, shredded mozzarella cheese and
Wildtree Mesquite Smoked Sun-Dried Tomato & Leek Blend*

*Crushed tomatoes, shredded mozzarella cheese and
Wildtree Red Bell Pepper & Garlic Blend*

Goat cheese and Wildtree Garlic & Herb Blend

*Crushed tomatoes, shredded mozzarella cheese and chopped cooked chicken
that has been marinated in Wildtree Asian Ginger-Plum Dressing & Marinade*

*Wildtree Sun-Dried Tomato Pesto,
shredded mozzarella cheese and grated Parmesan cheese*

Quick-Quick Pizza

Serves 4

1 pound pizza dough
1 tablespoon Wildtree Roasted Garlic Grapeseed Oil
2 plum tomatoes, sliced
1 tablespoon Wildtree Hearty Spaghetti Sauce Blend
1/3 cup grated Parmesan cheese

Roll the pizza dough into a circle on a floured surface. Brush with the Roasted Garlic Grapeseed Oil.

Arrange the tomato slices on the prepared dough. Top with the Hearty Spaghetti Sauce Blend and sprinkle with the cheese.

Bake at 400 degrees for 15 minutes.

Wildtree Tip: *Try making this with foccacia bread instead of the pizza dough.*

santa fe pizza

Serves 4

3 tablespoons Wildtree Natural Grapeseed Oil
1 teaspoon Wildtree Mesquite Smoked Sun-Dried Tomato & Leek Blend
1 boneless skinless chicken breast
1 pound pizza dough
1 tablespoon Wildtree Natural Grapeseed Oil
1 plum tomato, sliced
1 green onion, sliced
Cilantro
Chopped olives
Shredded Monterey Jack cheese
Sour cream (optional)
Guacamole (optional)
Wildtree Chunky Style Salsa

Combine 3 tablespoons Grapeseed Oil and the Mesquite Smoked Sun-Dried Tomato & Leek Blend in a bowl. Coat the chicken with the mixture and grill over hot coals until cooked through. Chop the chicken.

Roll the pizza dough into a circle on a floured surface. Brush 1 tablespoon Grapeseed Oil on the dough. Layer the chicken, tomato and green onion on the prepared dough. Sprinkle with cilantro, olives and cheese.

Bake at 400 degrees for 10 to 12 minutes. Serve with sour cream, guacamole and Wildtree Chunky Style Salsa.

Red Pepper & Garlic Pizza
Serves 4

1 tablespoon Wildtree Red Bell Pepper & Garlic Blend
1 pound pizza dough
1 tablespoon Wildtree Basil Pesto Grapeseed Oil or Wildtree Roasted Garlic Grapeseed Oil
1 red bell pepper, sliced, or 1 plum tomato, sliced
2 ounces prosciutto, thinly sliced
2 ounces gorgonzola cheese or feta cheese, crumbled
4 ounces spinach or broccoli rabe, cooked and chopped

Rehydrate the Red Bell Pepper & Garlic Blend using the package directions. Roll the pizza dough into a circle on a floured surface. Brush the dough with the Basil Pesto Grapeseed Oil. Brush with the Red Bell Pepper & Garlic Blend.

Top with the bell pepper and prosciutto. Sprinkle with the cheese and top with the spinach. Bake at 400 degrees for 15 to 20 minutes.

Quick White Pizza
Serves 4

1 tablespoon Wildtree Scampi Blend
1 teaspoon water
3 tablespoons Wildtree Natural Grapeseed Oil
1 pound pizza dough
1/3 cup freshly grated Parmesan cheese

Combine the Scampi Blend with the water in a small bowl and mix until of a paste consistency. Add the Natural Grapeseed Oil and mix well.

Roll the pizza dough into a circle on a floured surface. Brush the dough with the Scampi Blend mixture. Sprinkle with half the cheese. Bake at 400 degrees for 8 to 12 minutes. Sprinkle with the remaining cheese just before serving. You may sprinkle with chopped flat-leaf parsley if desired.

basic pasta sauce

Serves 4

1 (28-ounce) can crushed tomatoes
1 tablespoon Wildtree Hearty Spaghetti Sauce Blend

Combine the tomatoes and Hearty Spaghetti Sauce Blend in a saucepan and simmer for 20 minutes. Serve over your choice of pasta.

Wildtree Tip: *Substitute Wildtree Garden Vegetable Pasta Sauce Blend, Wildtree Red Bell Pepper & Onion Pasta Sauce Blend, or Wildtree Porcini Mushroom & Toasted Onion Pasta Sauce Blend for the Hearty Spaghetti Sauce Blend.*

Try adding your favorite Pasta or Spaghetti Sauce Blend to meatballs, burgers or meat loaf. Use to flavor bread crumbs, or knead into prepared bread dough and bake as usual.

For added flavor, add to stews, braised meats or pot roast.

For a simple salad dressing, add to oil, vinegar, salt and pepper.

Blend 1 tablespoon Wildtree Garden Vegetable Pasta Sauce with 1 cup cottage cheese. Refrigerate for 1 hour before serving.

sugar & *Spice*

CREAM CHEESE SQUARES

Serves 12 to 16

2 (8-count) packages crescent rolls
16 ounces cream cheese, softened
1 (.8-ounce) package Wildtree Pumpkin Cheesecake Blend
3/4 cup sugar
1/2 cup confectioners' sugar
2 teaspoons milk
Dash of vanilla extract

Layer 1 package of crescent rolls in a 9x13-inch glass baking dish, pressing the edges together to form 1 layer. Combine half the cream cheese with the Pumpkin Cheesecake Blend and sugar in a bowl and mix until blended. Spread over the crescent roll layer. Spread with the remaining cream cheese. Top with the remaining crescent rolls, pressing the edges together to form the top layer.

Bake at 325 to 350 degrees for 25 minutes or until golden brown.

Combine the confectioners' sugar, milk and vanilla in a bowl and mix well. Drizzle over the warm baked layer. Cut into squares.

Wildtree Tip: *This recipe can be made with any of the Wildtree Cheesecake Blends.*

apple crisp

Serves 6

5 McIntosh apples, peeled and sliced
2 teaspoons Wildtree Apple Pie Spice Blend
1/3 cup butter, softened
1/3 cup sugar
1/3 cup flour

Arrange the apples in a buttered 8x8-inch glass baking dish. Sprinkle with the Apple Pie Spice Blend. Combine the butter, sugar and flour in a bowl and mix well. Spread over the apples.

Bake at 350 degrees for 30 to 45 minutes or until the apples are soft and the topping is golden brown.

Serve warm or at room temperature with ice cream or whipped cream.

vanilla sugar

Makes 2 cups

2 cups sugar
1 Wildtree Vanilla Bean

Process the sugar and Vanilla Bean in a food processor until the Vanilla Bean is finely minced. Strain the sugar, discarding any large pieces of the Vanilla Bean. Store in an airtight container.

Wildtree Tip: *Use to add a fresh-tasting vanilla flavor to all of your favorite recipes. This is really good when used to sweeten whipped cream.*

BROWNIES WITH CHOCOLATE FUDGE SAUCE AND ICE CREAM

Serves 16

¹/₂ cup (1 stick) butter
4 ounces unsweetened chocolate
1 ¹/₂ teaspoons vanilla extract
1 ³/₄ cups sugar
2 eggs
1 cup flour
1 cup chopped pecans (optional)
Wildtree Rich Dark Chocolate Fudge Sauce
Ice cream

Melt the butter in a saucepan over very low heat. Stir in the unsweetened chocolate until melted. Remove from the heat and let stand for 10 minutes. Add the vanilla. Stir in the sugar gradually. Add the eggs 1 at a time, beating well after each addition. Stir in the flour and pecans gradually. Spoon into a greased and floured 9x9-inch baking pan.

Bake at 350 degrees for 30 minutes. Remove to a wire rack to cool completely. Cut the brownies into squares and place on dessert plates.

Spoon Rich Dark Chocolate Fudge Sauce into a microwave-safe bowl. Microwave until heated through. Pour over the brownies. Serve each with a scoop of ice cream.

> ***Wildtree Tip:*** *Substitute Wildtree Merlot Chocolate Fudge Sauce, Wildtree Pinot Grigio Chocolate Fudge Sauce or Wildtree Raspberry Chocolate Fudge Sauce for the Rich Dark Chocolate Fudge Sauce.*

fondue

Makes a variable amount

Your choice of
Wildtree Raspberry Chocolate Fudge Sauce,
Wildtree Merlot Chocolate Fudge Sauce,
Wildtree Pinot Grigio Chocolate Fudge Sauce or
Wildtree Rich Dark Chocolate Fudge Sauce
Whole strawberries
Melon chunks
Pineapple chunks
Pound cake, angel food cake or sponge cake cubes

Melt Fudge Sauce in a fondue pot over a low flame. Dip the strawberries, melon, pineapple and cake into the sauce using a fork. Use any combination of seasonal fruit for a quick and delicious dessert.

Wildtree Tip: *Melt and drizzle your favorite flavor of Wildtree Fudge Sauce on cheesecake, flan, mousse, or waffles and top with whipped cream, or use in parfaits or trifles with custard or pudding. Dunk biscotti or shortbread cookies in melted Wildtree Fudge Sauce.*

NO-Bake Wildtree Lemon Lime Cheesecake

Serves 8

16 ounces cream cheese, softened
8 ounces whipped topping
1 (.8-ounce) package Wildtree Lemon Lime Cheesecake Blend
1 graham cracker pie shell
Sliced lemons and limes (optional)

Combine the cream cheese, whipped topping and Lemon Lime Cheesecake Blend in a mixing bowl and beat until blended. Spoon into the pie shell. Chill, covered, for 2 hours or longer. Garnish with lemon and lime slices.

Wildtree Tip: *You may substitue any of the Wildtree Cheescake Blends for the Lemon Lime Cheescake Blend.*

CONVERSIONS

3 teaspoons	1 tablespoon
2 tablespoons	1/8 cup
4 tablespoons	1/4 cup
5 tablespoons plus 1 teaspoon	1/3 cup
8 tablespoons	1/2 cup
12 tablespoons	3/4 cup
16 tablespoons	1 cup
32 tablespoons	2 cups
64 tablespoons	1 quart
96 tablespoons	1 1/2 quarts
1 ounce	2 tablespoons fat or liquid
4 ounces	1/2 cup
8 ounces	1 cup
16 ounces	1 pound
5/8 cup	1/2 cup plus 2 tablespoons equals 10 tablespoons
7/8 cup	3/4 cup plus 2 tablespoons equals 14 tablespoons
2 cups	1 pint
2 pints	1 quart
1 quart	4 cups
4 quarts	1 gallon

INDEX

PRODUCT INDEX

Wildtree Herbs, Inc.

11 Knight Street

Warwick, Rhode Island 02886

401-732-1856

www.wildtreeherbs.com

WILDTREE HERBS